knockings at my heart

In memory of
Rabindranath Tagore's
first visit to Japan
in 1916.

knockings at my heart

UNPUBLISHED POEMS OF
RABINDRANATH TAGORE

COMPILED AND EDITED BY
NILANJAN BANERJEE

WITH ILLUSTRATIONS BY
K.G. SUBRAMANYAN

LOTUS COLLECTION
ROLI BOOKS

Lotus Collection, 2016

© Introduction: Nilanjan Banerjee
    Illustrations: K.G. Subramanyan

ISBN: 978-93-5194-106-4

The Lotus Collection
An imprint of
Roli Books Pvt. Ltd.
M-75, G.K. II Market
New Delhi 110 048
Phone: ++91-011-40682000
Fax: ++91-11-2921 7185
E-mail: info@rolibooks.com
Website: www.rolibooks.com
Also at
Bangaluru, Chennai, and Mumbai

Cover: Sneha Pamneja
Calligraphy: Amit Kharsani

Printed and bound at Nutech Print Services-India

Contents

Introduction

Rabindranath Tagore (1861-1941) was born in one of the most prominent families of Bengal. The Tagores were Pirali Brahmins who had taken the lead to engage in trade with the English and the household brought together a confluence of Indian, European and Persian culture during the lifetime of Dwarakanath Tagore and Maharshi Debendranath Tagore. The household was a hub of creativity and experimentation when Rabindranath was born.

Rabindranath Tagore's formal school education remained incomplete. He was educated at home primarily by house tutors, after briefly attending three public schools in Calcutta without much success. The curriculum, at home, included English and he confidently attempted to translate William Shakespeare's *Macbeth* at the age of twelve. Like several of his early writings, his translation of *Macbeth* was lost.

Rabindranath wrote primarily and extensively in Bengali. He gradually went on to become a powerful bilingual writer, translating several of his literary pieces into English. Prior to his visit to England in 1912, he translated a selection of his Bengali poems which resulted in his maiden anthology of devotional songs and poems, *Gitanjali*. Rabindranath, after his arrival in London, shared his translations with his friend, the British portrait painter William Rothenstein. Rothenstein prepared three copies of the manuscript and sent them to William Butler Yeats, Stopford Brooke, and A.C. Bradley for comments.

Yeats suggested minor modifications to Rabindranath's translations and the India Society of London published *Gitanjali* in 1912. Yeats wrote an Introduction to the book, elucidating that Rabindranath's prose translations 'stirred' his blood even without knowing the 'movements of thought that have made them possible.' He went on to write, 'These lyrics ... display in their thought I have dreamed of all my life long.' With these words Yeats not only praised Rabindranath's outstanding poetic genius, but also his qualities as a translator. However, it may be noted that much later in 1935, Yeats would comment, 'Tagore does not know English, no Indians know English.'[1]

Gitanjali brought Rabindranath the Nobel Prize in Literature in 1913. Ten subsequent editions of *Gitanjali* were published in London between March and November of 1913. Rabindranath's sudden exposure to global limelight, widely and steadily, demanded translations of his works and he himself took much interest in translating some of his literary pieces into English. As a result, several of his books were published in English (in his own English translations and few others originally written in English), which included: *The Gardener* (poems, 1913), *Sadhana* (essays and lectures, 1913), *The Crescent Moon* (child–poems, 1913), *Chitra* (drama, 1913), *Fruit-Gathering* (poems, 1916), *Sacrifice and Other Plays* (1917), *Nationalism* (essays, 1917),

Personality (lectures delivered in America, 1917), *Lover's Gift and Crossings* (poems and songs, 1918), *The Parrot's Training* (allegorical satire, 1918), *Creative Unity* (essays and lectures, 1922), *Talks in China* (addresses, 1925), The Child (poem, 1931), *The Religion of Man* (lectures, 1931), *Man* (lectures, 1931) and *Crisis in Civilization* (lecture, 1941).

Rabindranath's career as an English writer is restricted primarily to translations of his own Bengali works. His original English writings included lectures, addresses and numerous letters which were largely composed during his foreign travels or while corresponding with friends around the world.

His first known attempt to render his own poem appears to be 'Desire for a Human Soul', an incomplete English translation of 'Nisphal Kamana' in the manuscript of *Manashi* (1890). Rabindranath's poems, written originally in English are very few, including his major English poem 'The Child' (1931). He translated this poem into Bengali as 'Sisu Tirtha' which was included in his book *Punascha* in 1932. Scholars have identified a poem ('The lamp is trimmed/Comrades, bring your own fire to light it...') as the first poem written in English by Rabindranath in 1918. This poem was written to support a fund-raising campaign for the Society for the Promotion of National Education in celebrating the National Education Week in Adyar, Madras. Discussing this poem, Rabindranath wrote to James H. Cousins in a letter that, 'The message I sent for the National Education Week is not twice born. It was written for the occasion in English at the instigation of Mr Arundale [George Arundale].'

Rabindranath composed numerous short poems during his visits to China and Japan between 1916 and 1929. The Nobel Prize for Literature had made him a celebrity in Asia and Europe and he was often requested by enthusiasts to compose short poems while signing autographs, a craft that Rabindranath perfected. While many of these autograph-poems were written in Bengali with English translations, he wrote a few others directly into English without any Bengali translation. During his visit to Europe in 1926, he arranged a selection of these poems in his own calligraphy for a bilingual book of epigrammatic verses, titled *Lekhan*. The book was printed in Germany in 1926 and published in India the following year. *Stray Birds* (1916) and *Fireflies* (1928) were two other books published during the lifetime of the poet compiling his short verses, most of which had been composed as autograph-poems. Rabindranath used to modify his literary works at frequent intervals, producing several versions of the same creative pieces in the process. Multiple versions of Rabindranath's autograph-poems can be found either in the poet's own handwriting or in typed scripts or printed forms.

This is a compilation of some unpublished autograph-poems of Rabindranath from the archives of Rabindra-Bhavana at Visva-Bharati. The file 'MSF Autograph Poems' at Rabindra-Bhavana contains several sets of typed poems of Rabindranath. A few of these pages are typewritten drafts with handwritten corrections and revisions by the poet himself. The other poems seem to be the final typed copies without any modifications. The file 'MS 460' includes eight poems by Rabindranath in his own handwriting in an address book. Some postal addresses were also jotted down by him in some pages of the largely unused notebook.

Rabindranath Tagore reiterated his thoughts and ideas in his poems, essays, speeches, songs, letters and also in his manuscript doodles and paintings. Hence, it would be difficult to ascertain whether these poems were written directly in English or they were 'twice born', being English translations of their Bengali originals. Rabindranath was influenced by the precision, depth, power, and intensity of Japanese haiku poetry and took his autograph-poems seriously. This is evident in the painstaking modification of many of these poems years after they had been written and published.

Rabindranath was never ambitious to be known as an 'English' poet in any sense of the term. Neither did he continue to translate his own works simultaneously and constantly with his original creations in Bengali, presumably because he felt that '... it is never the function of a poet to personally help in transportation of his poems to an alien form and atmosphere...'[2] These sporadic short verses of Rabindranath that remain undated, were possibly written in response to specific public demands and not so much out of any urge to express himself in a language with its 'strictly guarded boundaries'.[3]

NOTES

1. *The Letters of W.B. Yeats*, edited by Allan Wade, London, 1954.
2. See Rabindranath's letter to Amiya Chakraborty on 26 November 1932, in Bikash Chakraborty, *Ingrijite Rabindranath o Anyanna* (in Bengali), Puascha, Kolkata, 2010, p. 46.
3. Bikash Chakraborty, *Ingrijite Rabindranath o Anyanna* (in Bengali), Puascha, Kolkata, 2010, p. 47.

Beauty smiles in the bud,
in its perfect incompleteness.

Break the difference
and it is multiplied.

Children run out of the temple
and play in the dust.
God watches their games
and forgets the priest.

Devil's wares are expensive
God's gifts are priceless.

God among stars
waits for man
to light his lamp.

God watches the single night
of a firefly
and the agelong night
of the star.

I hear the knockings at my
heart of the morning's hopes
sadly coming back
at the night.

Let him take note of the thorn
who can see the flower
as a whole.

Life's tapestry is woven
by the joining and breaking
of its threads.

Love whose loss is forgotten
is like a dumb hour
that has no bird's songs
but only cricket's chirp.

Mind, like a brook,
starts up at a sudden liquid note
of its own
that is never repeated.

My migratory songs are on wings
seeking their nests in thy voice.

My offerings are spent
at the wayside shrines,
I bring my emptiness to the Temple.

Thy untuned strings beg for music in their anguished discord.

Thy words that are slight
may lightly dance upon time's waves
while my words heavy with import
sink.

The reward of my work is in daily wages, in love of my own final value.

Since she has vanished from my reach
the wind carries the rustle of her movements
among the restless grass.

Spring in pity for the desolate branch
left one fluttering kiss in a solitary leaf.

The ancient light is ever young,
the shadow of the moment is born old.

The bubble doubts the sea
and its laugh burst into emptiness.

The day offers to the silence of night
his golden lute be tuned.

The day's glare of curiosity
makes the stars shrink
and disappear.

The distance came near to me
in the morning
and came still nearer
when taken away by the night.

The earth in the sunset glow
seems like a ripe fruit
ready to be gathered by the night.

The fist that doubts its wisdom
throttles the voice that would cry.

The fist throttles truth
to silence the doubt
of its own wisdom.

The man proud of his sect
thinks that he has the sea
ladled into his
own private pond.

The mist tries to capture the
morning
in a foolish persistence.

The one in its solitude is emptiness,
the other one gives it truth.

The pomegranate bud hidden
behind her veil
will burst into passionate flowers
when I am away.

The wind brings the call,
the anchor clutches the mud,
the boat beats its breast
against the chain.

The worm thinks it foolish
that man does not eat his books.

They build a cage and claim thanks
for the security it offers.

Thou art late, my crescent moon,
but my night bird is awake to greet you.

Thou hast left to the lonely lamp
thy memory in a flame.

To bear the cost of the instrument
and never to know that it is
for the music
is the tragedy of life's deafness.

Too ready to blame the bad,
too reluctant to praise the good.

Truth smiles in beauty
when she beholds her face
in a perfect mirror.

Upon the ruins of tyrant's triumph
children build their dust castle.

When dawn, the many-coloured flower,
fades
the sun as its fruit comes out
in a simple white light.

Wishing to hearten a timid lamp
the great night lights all her stars.

Across the illimitable hush of time—
rings the march music of man.

This morning I have my singer's errand to the birthday feast of the honeysuckle.

I am the south wind that
do not claim honey from the flower,
but only its faint timid whisper.

In your kiss, my love,
all my tomorrows merge
in an endless today.

Why go through life like a child
who turns the pages of a book
and believes that this is reading?

May the desolate ghost of the forgotten
cease crying to find back its body.

The daisy watches the sun
opening out from the dusk
and longs to rival it.

Praise frightens me
lest it be proved my debt.

I ever wonder when I am before thee,
why I were not made like a forest
that opens its heart in flowers,
like a star in its speech of flame.

My love longs to offer its worship in splendour
but poor are its vessels in me
Let me leave it to her to celebrate love's feast
whose beauty is lighted with its own bliss,
whose smile is a boon.

Gods are amused when the busy river
condemns the cloud as an unpractical dream.

God would remain imperfect
if he could not at the same time be a man.

Freedom is not gained through the broken walls,
it is captured through the open windows.

The large laughter of the morning
is blurred by the miserly mist into a sneer.

The man of business claims
    from the tree its building plan,
and laughs when the tree looks foolish.

The mediocre in power barricades himself with wholesale suspicion against risks which his stupidity cannot define.

The coward is terribly indiscriminate.

The god of the weak is tyrant.

The slave is busy
making whips for his master.

Tiredness comes as a bride
    to the unyielding strength
to kiss it into a surrender.

Let me own my defeat to thee my sweet,
and win thee in return.

A woman noxious, is vain of her venom
She not only bites but hisses in exultation .

A gourmet in gossip uses
indignation as a spice
to enjoy vicarious vice.

The devil has his advantage
over the divine powers
for, it is easy to heart and
bafflingly hard to heal.

The savagery of slander poisons with
lies the arrow-tips of broken facts
to make them meanly perfect.

The meaning of the seed
    waits in the heart of time.
But what is time?

The importunate wave pushes away
the fruit it longs to capture.

The deserted path finds its veil
in the grass that decorates its neglect.

Let not my today leave
its tattered remnants
to narrow the passage of my tomorrow.

My dumb desire tells its beads
in the dusk of its loneliness
in a hermit's cell for my dreams.

The moutains dream of a golden age—
when they were birds with
wings and a voice.

Freedom is not overtaken through broken walls,
it is welcomed through open gates.

The storm that shattered my flower
has vanished
but the flower has not died in its death.

My nest-weary wings fluttered
in the hesitating dusk of dawn
when answer to the first faint whisper
of light in the East,
'Seek thy dwelling by the sea'
came the call,
'Where the earth's voices blend
into music
in the glad heart of the Silent.'

The conquering Spirit of Life has
only small blades of grass
For its weapon when it goes
to meet the mighty Demon of Desert.

Bigotry kills Truth in its savage effort to save it.

Let my life accept the risk of its sails and not merely the security of its anchor.

The sacrifice of leaves blossoms in flowers.

Truth when opposed becomes
conscious of its triumphant self.

They blame the fish for
having bones who wants to
swallow it.

K.G. Subramanyan, born in Kerala in 1924, is one of the pioneers of Indian modern art. He taught at Kala-Bhawan of Visva-Bharati and MS University of Baroda over decades. He was awarded the Padma Vibhushan by the Government of India in 2012.

Nilanjan Banerjee was educated at Visva-Bharati of India and Reitaku University of Japan. He is a poet, painter, curator, and film maker with a series of publications to his credit. A Charles Wallace Scholar, he was trained as a curator by the British Museum, UK.